I Can Fix It!

Written by Caroline Harris
Illustrated by Neil Sutherland, Blue-Zoo and Tony Trimmer

O is sad. X can fix it!

o-**x**, ox!
It is an ox!

F links up.

f-o-x, fox!

S and I pop in.

1, 2, 3, 4, 5 ... 6!
Six foxes!

Can I fix it?

m-i-x, mix!
It is a big mix-up!

The foxes get into a mess.

It is no fun!
It must stop!

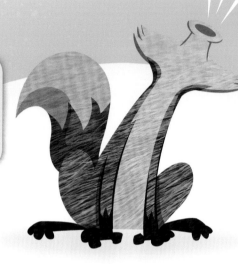

o!

X has a plan!

b-o-x, box!
X gets the foxes into
a big box!